THE WITCH'S TALE

KERRY MITCHELL

A Birdy Black Book

Copyright © 2018 by **Kerry Mitchell**

All rights reserved. No part of this publication may be reproduced, distributed or transmitted in any form or by any means, without prior written permission.

Birdy Black Books
Melbourne

Publisher's Note: This is a work of fiction. Names, characters, places, and incidents are a product of the author's imagination. Locales and public names are sometimes used for atmospheric purposes. Any resemblance to actual people, living or dead, or to businesses, companies, events, institutions, or locales is completely coincidental.

Book Layout © 2017 BookDesignTemplates.com
Printed by Ingram Spark USA

The Witch's Tale/ Kerry Mitchell. -- 1st ed.
ISBN 978-0-6482301-1-3

I am the power, I am the force
The bravest knight on the swiftest horse

I am the fire in the dragon's eye
I am the maiden and hero am I

I am the strength my hero commands
I am the wish in the far-away lands

I am the dark in the dead of the night
I am the fearless, I am the fright

I am the beauty, I am the beast
I am the nourishment of the feast

I am the promise of a new day dawning
Eye of the storm, I am the warning

I am the beginning, I am the end
The story of old, real or pretend

I am eternal, the legend, the lore
I am the memory of it all

CONTENTS

SPINNING STRAW INTO GOLD 1
THE PRINCESS IN THE TOWER 13
THE SLEEPING LUCY 19
LUCY AND THE BEAST 25
THE GINGERBREAD HOUSE 31
THE BLUE-EYED BUNNY 35
HALLOWEEN WITCHES 47
CROW! 53
THE UGLIEST OF ALL 59
LUCY LAURA LOCKET 63
THE SAD, SAD TALE OF ABIGAIL 67
CINDER-ELLA 77
PRINCESS POLLY AND THE PEA 83
PRUNELLA 93

TALE ONE

SPINNING STRAW INTO GOLD

Once upon a time in the Kingdom of Grim
There was a Miller on his way to the King

The air was hazy, as if in a dream
As the Miller stopped for a drink by a stream

He knelt by the water, he was thirsty I suppose
When he suddenly spied the most beautiful rose

He thought of his daughter, whom he sorely missed
And snatched the rose into his fist

When just at that moment, right out of the blue
The King came riding into view

His nostrils flared, his eyes turned black
It looked as though he might attack

'Is that a rose that you have found?
How dare you pluck it from the ground!

Every petal, every stalk
As far as anyone can walk

Belongs to me, you understand
For you are standing on my land!'

The King was furious, you see
About as mad as one can be

And the Miller quickly fell to one knee
And said a little haltingly

'S-s-sire, I beg you, spare my life
And in return, I'll give you a wife'

The King rubbed his chin, and furrowed his brow
He would have whistled but he didn't know how
So he thought a sigh would suffice for now

He looked at the Miller and his eyes he crossed
Accidentally, of course, he was feeling lost

But he thought the Miller had argued his case
And besides, the rose would have just gone to waste

So resting his horse by the shade of a tree
He granted the Miller full immunity

Whilst he hashed out the details of the deal
He finally offered the Miller a meal

They went to the pub for a pint of ale
But passed on the bread, it was lumpy and stale

The Miller, a man true to his word
Was hoping his offer the King hadn't heard

But the King was eager to secure a wife
So he thought it was fair to spare the man's life

'But why should I choose your daughter's hand
When I can have any girl in the land?'

The Miller was afraid the King would renege
And probably try to break his leg

So he came up with a plan, he thought it a beaut
To make his daughter seem more cute

'Sire,' he said, 'if the truth be told
I have a daughter who spins straw into gold'

Now this wasn't true, wasn't true at all
And already the Miller was starting to pall

But he'd blurted it out in a bid to impress
Let's not forget he was under duress

And the King, for his part, seemed keen to pursue
A woman like that, well, wouldn't you?

So he gave the Miller not a chance to retract
And took what he said to be matter of fact

'Make it so,' said the King, as he mounted his steed
'But there's no cause to rush, take as long as you need

Have your daughter at Castle upon my return
I like a woman whose keep she can earn'

Then the King rode off with his steed and his servant
His advisors and guards, looking fevered and fervent

His swords and his armour, his flags and his banner…
To await the arrival of the daughter, Diana

And the Miller was left wishing he'd had a son
And dreading telling Diana what he'd done

But she, for her part, seemed gracious and giving
And lucky for the Miller, was kind and forgiving

She was sure the King would not hold a grudge
When he saw that she'd spun her straw into sludge

Surely a man of such high social standing
Wouldn't be so mean and demanding?

Oh Diana, you fool, if that were only true
But the King was not as gracious as you

Though royal and regal, if truth be told
The King was greedy and wanted more gold

So Diana was led shortly thereafter
To a room with straw filled to the rafter

With door bolted shut and barricaded to boot
Diana was left to spin straw into loot

And just for a little added incentive
The King, for his part, had become quite inventive

He decreed that if Diana had no gold come morning
He would, and at this point the King started yawning

He would have her beheaded just for a lark...
Diana sat alone in the dark

She sat for a long time not saying a word
Til a little sob was finally heard

And at that moment there came a flash and a bang
And before her stood a strange little man

'What will you give,' said the man, feeling bold
'If I spin all this straw into gold?'

Said Diana, feeling desperate and glum
'I'll give you anything you want, old chum'

Then, hoping he didn't want to be kissed
'How about this bracelet on my wrist?'

'Done,' said the man and he sat on the floor
And started to spin into gold all that straw

By morning the glorious gold had been threaded
And Diana felt sure that now they'd be wedded
(With no more talk of her being beheaded)

But the King was greedy beyond compare
He wanted gold and more than his share

Another night, another room, as we all feared
But again the strange little man reappeared

This time a necklace was paid in advance
And by morning the King was doing a dance

But wanting an even bigger parcel
Diana was placed in the biggest room in the castle

Now I know this seems an awful shame
But the little man found her just the same

He asked her again what she would pay
But this time Diana knew not what to say

The poor girl couldn't even beg, borrow or steal
There was nothing left to make a deal

But the strange little man had a strange little plan for he was not one to be defeated
'Give me your first-born child,' said he, 'and this task shall be completed'

Diana was not even sure that this task would end in matrimony
She was beginning to think that the King was nothing but a big phoney

And, besides, a child was a long way away
She was sure to think of a plan someday

To save the child as yet unborn
And so the straw was spun by morn

With three rooms now filled to the brim
There was finally enough gold in the Kingdom of Grim

The King and Diana were married at dawn
And nine months later Lucinda was born

The Princess was barely a month or two old
When the strange little man who'd spun straw into gold

Arrived to claim his promised prize
Taking the Queen by complete surprise

She begged, she pleaded, offered jewels and gold
But all this left the little man cold

He was not interested in any of that lot
Diana was about to faint on the spot

When the man took pity and offered an out
Though goodness knows what that was about

Perhaps he thought his plan was foolproof
Alas, if only he'd known the truth!

He said to Diana, 'My Queen, do not weep
If you guess my name, your baby you'll keep

You have three days, guess as much as you like
But if you fail, I'm keeping the tyke'

Diana grew desperate and started to wail
She knew this task she must not fail

She sent her servants to travel the land
To identify the strange little man

She searched the library, she read every book
She was willing to take whatever it took

She made a list ten metres wide
And even used names of people who'd died

She said she hadn't but she lied
'He must be on this list,' she cried

Then, before she knew what more to do
The little man popped into view

Diana began with a little nod
Starting with the strange and odd

'Is it Guzzleguts? Is it Twinkletoes?
Or Rancidbreath, I don't suppose?'

But with every name, he shook his head
And at the end he simply said

'Two more days'
And disappeared in a cloudy haze

The second day was repeated to the letter
And sadly the outcome was no better

From Abraham and Albert, to Zachary and Zeke
The outcome still was looking bleak

When just before dawn on day number three
A witch arrived, that's right – me!

'I have news, Your Majesty,' I said
Bowing low my witchy head

'Whilst walking through the forest damp
I came upon a strange man's camp

The little man was leaping high
And letting out a joyful cry

He kept repeating, again and again
Simply the most peculiar name'

Said Diana, 'This name is what I yearn
What can I give you in return?'

Now it's true my beauty is quite rare
The likes of which cannot compare

And needing neither fame nor wealth
I desired the baby for myself

But not intending any malice
I promised to raise her in the palace

In a tower high in the Kingdom of Grim
The girl would serve my every whim

And any time the child was missed
The Queen could visit whenever she wished

Diana agreed, though she was vexed
So I explained what happened next

'He did not seem like normal folk
And this is what the strange man spoke:

"The Queen will never guess, it's plain
That Rumpelstiltskin is my name."'

The Queen's eyes popped, her mouth flew open
She said, 'Good grief, you must be jokin'!'
But when that night the strange man came
She knew that now she had his name
(But first she planned to play a game)

When he asked his name, she politely guessed
Planning to leave til last the best

'Is it Summersault? Is it Peppermint?
I would so appreciate a hint

Is it…' and here Diana hesitated
And eyed the man as he patiently waited

'Is it Rumpelstiltskin, could it be?'
The Queen enquired so innocently

The little man let out a howl
Someone offered him a towel

He stamped his foot right through the floor
And he was not seen anymore

There have been rumours, I must admit
That in my tower he'd sometimes sit

But would I have hatched this wicked scheme
Just to trick our lovely Queen?

Of course, some things you just can't tell
But everything will turn out well….

TALE TWO

THE PRINCESS IN THE TOWER

Lucinda was shipped off to the tower
And forced to live under my (awesome) power

Of course as a baby she didn't do much
Just a little light dusting and cooking and such

But magic exists in a higher state
And before too long she was pulling her weight

She grew quite quickly, hardy and strong
And did all the work before too long

She washed, she scrubbed, she cooked, she swept
And late at night whilst others slept

I went outside to explore
There were no stairs, there was no door

But Lucy's hair, like most teenagers
Was growing out in many stages

She liked it long, there is no doubt
And that is how I got out

To get back in, I called above:
'Let your hair down, Love!'

The King and Queen did not seem to mind
That the secret entrance they could not find

They had a son and lived in the castle
At birthdays and Christmas they sent a parcel

The Queen would visit and shout up to her daughter
Motherly advice like, 'Drink more water!'

Lucy ignored her mum's advice
She only listened once or twice

Then late one night whilst I was out witching
And Lucy sat in the tower stitching

It seemed an unseen power was guiding
When into the forest Prince Charming came riding

Lucy was singing a song so sweet
That the Prince knew they just had to meet

He hid in a bush and when I returned
The secret password he quickly learned

Next eve when I was out and about
Lucy heard a manly shout:

'Let your hair down, Love!'
And as he looked up, her hair fell from above

Although her hair was terribly knotted
The two quickly became besotted
(And her escape they secretly plotted)

Alas, one night as I climbed her hair
Lucy called out in despair

'You weigh a ton,' she said with a wince
'You're so much heavier than the Prince'

'What is this treachery?' I groaned
'I'm not heavy; I'm just big-boned!'

Once I'd gotten past the pain
I went over what was said again

The Prince? The Prince? How could this be?
How could he have gotten past GIGANTIC me?

I must admit I felt a bit peeved
And not just coz I'd been deceived

There was no need to call me names
And I was tired of their games

So in a fit of righteous rages
I grabbed the hair grown out in stages

And chopped it off, yes, to the ears
Lucy promptly collapsed in tears

Then she cried out with great glee
'Oh thank goodness I am free
That hair was simply stifling me!'

Lucy seemed to gain more strength
With every shortening of the length

'Listen here,' she said at last
'I'm sick of living in the past

No more being locked in towers
I wanna be free to smell the flowers'

There seemed no point to keep her there
Now I couldn't climb her hair

The Prince arrived from out of town
And got a ladder to help us down

Lucy might have broken the curse
But things were about to get much worse....

TALE THREE

THE SLEEPING LUCY

Lucy returned to the family palace
But her younger brother was terribly jealous

He'd had his parents all to his own
And didn't like it now she was home

Let it not be forgotten
Prince Harry was spoiled rotten

He convinced Lucy, though feeling sour
To follow him into another tower

And in this tower, frighteningly real
Sat an antiquated spinning wheel

I did a curse, yes, it's true
I guess you're thinking so what's new?

I'd be the last one to admit it
But let me tell you why I did it

When Lucy was born, they held a celebration
Inviting all throughout the nation

They even invited the coarse and unruly
Everyone, except yours truly

No one offered me a peek
I waited for the call all week

A lovely gift I had bought
But no one gave me a second thought

Was I hurt? Yeah, you bet
You know how sensitive I get

They said the invite had been mislaid
But by then my temper frayed

I ranted and raved and caused a scene
Cursing the Princess forever to dream

But when I calmed down, I allayed their fears
And only cursed for one hundred years

And the only way of breaking this
Was to receive her true love's kiss

If not, then her slumber would run out of breath
And the sleep would end in her ultimate death

A prick on the finger from a spinning wheel
And the curse would become a done deal

Prince Harry set the wheel in motion
All I did was conjure the potion

When Lucy pricked her little finger
Her brother decided not to linger

As she slept, the Palace wept
The King and Queen were most distressed

So I decided it would be best
If the entire Palace had a rest

Now I know this might sound alarming
But I even put to sleep Prince Charming

For one hundred years everyone dreamed
And nobody aged, or so it seemed

Prince after Prince arrived at the palace
And some of them were awfully zealous

But none could break the True Love Clause
I'm sorry folks but thems the laws

Whilst the others slept in their doona
I woke Prince Charming a little sooner

He had a head start by a couple of hours
Giving him a chance to pick flowers

Have a bite to eat and maybe a shower
Then get himself to the tower

Where he found Lucy in sweet repose
Gently snoring through her nose

He kissed her sweetly, her eyelids fluttered
'Oh no, not you again,' she muttered

She thought him cute, don't be mistaken
And was awfully glad to re-awaken

But Lucy's love for the Kingdom of Grim
Was not surprisingly growing thin

First, a strange man tried to take her away
And then she was locked in a tower all day

A jealous brother, an evil curse
Really, could things get any worse?

She went to the King and said, 'Listen Pop
This madness and mayhem has got to stop

I don't want to marry or settle down
And, Pop, I've gotta get out of this town'

'A Princess leave her palace and gold?'
The King was gob-smacked, if truth be told

'What will you do? You're a Princess, you know
You'll be hounded and bothered wherever you go'

Lucy smiled and kissed her dad
'Don't worry, things are not that bad

I'm sick of that witch ruining my life
She's brought me nothing but trouble and strife

I haven't decided on a whim
But it's time I left the Kingdom of Grim

I shall travel the land and tell my story
And leave nothing out, no matter how gory

Until everyone knows all about Diana
And the witch with a strange and unusual manner'

Diana looked sad but understood
'Don't get lost in the deep, dark wood

The witch might be hiding in there
Make sure you cover up your hair'

But things are not always as they seem
And a fairy tale can be just like a dream

The Princess must travel the world in disguise
Keeping secrets and one or two lies

And if the Princess's plan went without a hitch
Are you really sure that I'm the witch?

TALE FOUR

LUCY AND THE BEAST

Once upon a time in the Grim of old
Another story was set to unfold

It begins with a carriage, pulled by a horse
And the Princess running away, of course

Princess Lucy had reached the stage
Where she was sick of living in her gilded cage

So she hitched up her skirts and took off trotting
And a privileged life was soon forgotten

When travelling very far one day
She found a curious place to stay

A derelict castle, tattered and torn
Covered by thistle, thicket and thorn

She struggled inside out of the rain
But, surprisingly, no one came

Food was laid in the dining hall
But no one came to talk at all

She finished her meal, then looked about
She even gave a little shout

'Hi ho,' she called, 'is anyone home?'
Alas, the Princess was alone

She found a bed, cosy and warm
And fell asleep until the morn

Again, she was the only one
Where had all the others gone?

Food was once again supplied
'Where is everyone?' she cried

She stayed in the castle for almost a week
But no one ever came to speak

She felt a presence, that's for sure
But who it was she never saw

Until the day she went for a walk
And clearly heard a person talk

Behind a bush, hidden from view
A man said, 'Madam, how do you do?'

'I'm quite enchanted by this place
But why do you not show your face?'

'I cannot do so,' was his reply
'And I cannot tell you why

Please stay here and be my guest
It looks like you could use the rest'

Lucy agreed and did not push
To see the man behind the bush

Many times they'd sit and talk
Or through the garden they would walk

It didn't matter what they did
Still the man always hid

'I am a prince,' he confessed
'But I am not like all the rest

I have been cursed, to say the least
And now I have become… a beast!'

Lucy said, 'I don't care
I promise that I will not stare'

But the beast refused to budge
He couldn't bear to have her judge

And then one day something changed
He did not meet as they'd arranged

She could not find him anywhere
Lucy cried out in despair

'Beast, oh beast, where have you gone?
Without you, I cannot go on!'

It felt as though her heart would break
And it was more than she could take

She searched the castle and the ground
Until at last the beast was found

In the garden he was lying
It looked as though the beast was dying

She knelt beside the hideous creature
Taking in his every feature

Lucy tried hard not to stare
At the grizzled face and matted hair

She cradled him gently in her arm
Wondering who would do him harm

'Please, dear beast, do not go
Don't you know I love you so?'

She kissed his cheek and one tear fell
But maybe that was just as well

For it broke the curse and set him free
And things were just as they should be

The beast transformed back to the form
With which the Prince had first been born

And this is what was most alarming
The beast turned out to be Prince Charming!

'You again,' she said with a laugh
Helping the Prince up off the path

'It seems our destiny is fated
I'm awfully glad that you waited'

'It was the witch,' the Prince declared
'I'm only glad that you were spared

She turned her evil eye on me
And that is how I came to be

A beast, instead of what I am:
A good, upstanding, decent man

I love you, Lucy, can't you see
That you and I were meant to be?'

'Ooh, that witch!' Lucy seethed
'To think that I could be deceived

How could she do this to me again!
What has she got against you men?'

'Lucinda,' said the Prince at last
'Forget about our rocky past

She's done us a favour, for now I know
That I could never let you go

Life is short, there's no time to tarry
It's time that you and I did marry'

Everyone throughout the nation
Enjoyed the wedding celebration

And the whole affair went without a hitch
Because this time they remembered the witch

TALE FIVE

THE GINGERBREAD HOUSE

Once upon a time, oh you know how this goes
I can't stop now, I suppose

So, after the wedding I walked through the wood
To a shady spot where my cottage stood

'Peace at last,' I softly sighed
And quickly disappeared inside

Sometimes it's nice to get away
From all the troubles of the day

I take a nap, a gentle snooze
Or do whatever else I choose

But on this day in my hidden home
I discovered I was not alone

Outside a child had stopped to linger
And cautiously stretched out a finger

She swiped at the edge of the window pane
And surprise, surprise, it was candy cane

'Thank goodness,' she said, scratching at the carving
'I could do with a bite, I'm positively starving.'

She nibbled at the frosting, gave the candy a lick
And then ate the moulding til she felt quite sick

But the little blighter wanted more
So she started gnawing at my door

I shouted out, 'Get lost, you creep!
Can't you see I'm trying to sleep?'

But she said, 'Let me in, there's more food, I'm certain
Is that a cotton candy curtain?'

On reflection, although it's a shame
I suppose I have myself to blame

Who can resist a house of food?
But why do they have to be so rude?

I know I really shouldn't moan
But they're eating me out of house and home!

Those rotten kids just won't stop eating
And my house has taken quite a beating

So I did the only thing I could
And quickly hustled through the wood

In order to keep the house as mine
I hired workers to redesign

They soon came up with a brand new plan
And just as quickly as you can

They built another house for me
And this one, rather pleasingly

Was left alone by all those brats
It was even overlooked by rats

For underneath the hanging eaves
Was broccoli and cabbage leaves

The door was carrot sticks and gum
And as for sugar, not a one

Now that I'd conquered my sweet tooth
My house was healthy from floor to roof

And with every morsel gluten-free
There were no more kids to bother me

TALE SIX

THE BLUE-EYED BUNNY

Once upon a time, the King, it was said
Only needed a little bit of butter on his bread

But Queen Diana was a little bit funny
She preferred her bread smothered in honey

Lots of honey, lots and lots
It sat in the parlour in lots of pots

Until the day she ate every last one
And Diana was left feeling gloomy and glum

'What shall we do?' asked the King in despair
'We need to find more honey somewhere'

Now there was a maiden, clever and kind
And there wasn't a thing that she couldn't find

So she knew just what she had to do
To stop the Queen from feeling blue

She'd scour the land, the sea, the wood
And do the very best she could

She once found a needle in a stack of hay
And a pot of gold on a sunny day

She would find that honey, it would be such fun
And the Queen would no longer be feeling glum

So the maiden set off into the wood
Wearing a jacket with a red hood

Clouds rolled over the bright, warm sun
And in an instant the light was gone

Inside the wood, she became quite lost
But determined to press on at any cost

When suddenly the path was barred up ahead
And the maiden's heart filled with dread

For there I stood, dressed all in black
And the silly girl feared I would attack

'Where are you going?' I politely enquired
'Perhaps you should rest, you look quite tired'

'I can't,' said the maiden, 'I'm on a quest
And I don't have time to stop and rest

I'm looking for honey, a pot or two
And I don't have time to talk to you!'

The way that she was talking to me
Was a little bit rude, wouldn't you agree?

But still I obligingly stood aside
As the maiden ran on through the wooded wild

She stumbled through the thorny trees
Until she came upon some bees

The bees were gathered in a drone
By a little cottage made of stone

By the time the maiden rang the bell
I was also there as well

Hidden behind a bee-keeper's veil
I offered a pot of honey for sale

The girl didn't notice anything funny
And so she tasted the poisoned honey

But before she'd even paid her money
The maiden was turned into a bunny!

That's right, the little twerp was bewitched
And in an instant her body switched

But before I could inflict further wrath
A bee-keeper came down the path

Thinking fast, I quickly hid
And this is what the bee-keeper did:

His name was Barry and he lived alone
In that little cottage made of stone

He cared for the bees and he made fine honey
And was he surprised to find that bunny

He doesn't usually make a habit
Of getting acquainted with a rabbit

But her eyes were big and her fur was soft
So he scooped her up and then she coughed

He hoped she wasn't getting a cold
But I think she was, if truth be told

The bunny tried to hop away
She didn't seem to want to stay

But he held on tightly to her bod
And that's when he noticed something odd

Her eyes weren't brown, as they should have been
But the brightest blue he'd ever seen

'You're such a lovely bunny,' he said
As he kept her snuggly warm and fed

Then he took the bunny to meet his bees
But I was waiting behind the trees

I stood before him with a purse full of money
So naturally he thought I'd come to buy honey

I looked at the bunny and said, 'I've seen worse'
Then slowly opened up my purse

'How much are you asking, if I might avail?'
Said Barry, 'This bunny is not for sale'

'Of course I'll make it worth your while'
I responded with a friendly smile

I tried not to give the game away
But I was not in the mood to play

As the wind tangled up my hair
I gave Barry and his bunny a steely stare

'I mean you no harm,' I finally said
But those bees began to swarm round my head

So I waved my arms and gave a shout
'Give me that bunny!' I blurted out

'I won't!' he said, holding her tight
As day descended into night

In his arms she was kept
He even held her whilst he slept

Wherever he went, the bunny was there
Even into the village square

Down every path, at every gate
I would simply watch and wait

The days grew colder but, still alive
The bees remained inside their hive

Birds migrated by usual route
And the wandering gypsies followed suit

It happened to be a cold, crisp day
When a gypsy caravan came this way

Although its presence was only fleeting
Barry looked up and waved in greeting

Only when the wagon was out of sight
Did he notice that something was not quite right

A sack of grain had fallen out
Used to feed the horse, no doubt

And although the weather was getting colder
He placed the sack upon his shoulder

Still holding the bunny, Barry ran
Until he caught up with the gypsy van

'Hello,' he called, 'anyone about?'
And a gypsy lad poked his head out

'What is it you want?' he asked with suspicion
Barry quickly explained his mission

'Only to return this heavy sack
That fell from your wagon out the back'

'Oh, thanks,' said the gypsy, grabbing the sack
'I'm awfully glad to have that back'

Only then did he stop, only then did he stare
'My goodness,' he said, 'what have you got there?'

Barry stroked his bunny's paw
'Haven't you seen a bunny before?'

'Never one blue of eye'
Came the gypsy lad's reply

His grandmother he quickly sought
'Come see what this young man has brought'

A wizened woman with shoulders hunched
Back bent over and face all scrunched

Poked her head out of the van
And looked at the bunny, then at the man

'That is no bunny,' she said at last
'You've got yourself a girl with a past

She's been bewitched and it's not good'
It was then that Barry understood

He told the gypsies the strangest tale
Of a bunny that was not for sale

And how I'd appeared the very next day
And tried to take the bunny away

'You've not seen the last of that pesky witch'
Said the gypsy with a nervous twitch

'Halloween is upon us and as you know
That's when a witch's powers grow'

She paused then said, 'Listen, brother
One good turn deserves another

This wicked spell we can break
But we'll need your sleeping bees to wake'

The gypsy woman outlined a plan
Then home with the bunny Barry ran

On Hallow's Eve he went to his hive
Where the bees were thankfully still alive

He whispered low a magic charm
To keep the bees from further harm

The bees took flight and swarmed away
As slowly night engulfed the day

The gypsy van, led by the horse
Embarked upon its chosen course

Holding the bunny as tight as he could
On they rode into the wood

Never pausing as day turned to night
Keeping on track by the full moonlight

The plan, you see, was pretty clear
Barry would keep his bunny near

The bees would find my secret lair
And buzz about my tangled hair

If a spell I tried to cast
The bees would interfere real fast

Suddenly the bunny went berserk
And began to wriggle and twitch and jerk

Barry knew the midnight hour
Is when a witch has greatest power

I tried to take the hare from his hip
But Barry tightened up his grip

'Hands off my bunny,' he said with a growl
'I'll not be throwing in the towel!'

For a moment it seemed he spoke too soon
When dark clouds swept across the moon

But when the moon came into sight
Barry was still holding on tight

But instead of the bunny, he came face to face
With the beautiful maiden in its place

Still in his arms, she began to tell
How she came to be under my spell

'Against that witch I stood not a chance
I was simply a victim of circumstance'

It seems the situation was sorted
And all my evil plans were thwarted

Those pesky bees buzzed round my head
So that all my curses went unsaid

For a dozen times I was stung
And to my outer limits flung

The gypsies smiled, they knew the truth
An eye for an eye, a tooth for a tooth

Distraction is a handy tool
But do they take me for a fool?

I only meant to stir the pot
And this is all the thanks I got

How could they know if they were in love
Unless they were given a little shove?

I must have been doing something right
For things did change after that night

Barry and his bunny were soon in love
And thanked their lucky stars above

And shortly thereafter they were wed
'It's a dream come true,' the maiden said

She moved into the cottage made of stone
And quickly made herself at home

The maiden loved their simple life
And was happy to be a bee-keeper's wife

She cared for the bees and helped with the honey
And everybody called her Bunny

But best of all, it must be said
The Queen *always* had honey for her bread

TALE SEVEN

HALLOWEEN WITCHES

One Halloween night when the moon did not shine
And the wild wind howled most of the time

Three sister witches got together
In a little stone cottage, safe from the weather

Nestled inside a hollowed out grove
A big supper burbled and spat on the stove

Now all witches are not as sweet-natured as me
And these ones were about as mean as can be

They told tales about neighbours and lies about friends
And spells to be cast when the talking ends

'We'll take that girl, turn her into a toad

The one who was skipping across the road
She was bouncy and cheerful and sugary sweet
We'll squash her flat beneath our feet

And we'll take that boy who was riding his bike
And stick his head upon a spike

When those sickening children come trick or treating
We'll give those blighters such a beating

We'll poison their apples and make them sick
They want a treat but we'll give them a trick'

Outside the cottage I quietly stood
Having walked a long way through the wood

I heard the witches plot and scheme
And thought they were being terribly mean

So I knocked at the door, right out of the blue
And the witches called out, 'Who's there? Who?'

My voice rang out, clearly and bold
'A stranger, one who is hungry and cold'

The witches laughed and said, 'We're a-cookin
But just for us, you don't get a look-in!'

But my knocking kept on, steady and stout

Until in the end they just had to call out
'Who's that a-knockin?' And they looked all around
Then there came a wailing, whistling sound

'Let me in, do-oo
I'm cold through and thro-oo-ugh
And I'm hungry to-oo!'

The witches sang out, 'Go away, do
We're a-cookin for us; we'll not cook for you'

Then they sat by the fire and kept on eating
Same time my knocking kept on repeating

Now one of the witches, being a bit meek
Felt her resolve start to go weak

She decided a small piece of food was required
To give me what it was I desired

So she took a tiny piece of dough
About as big as your little toe

She took as small a piece as you can
And threw it into the frying pan

But as soon as the dough hit the frying pan
It began to swell again and again

It swelled over the pan, it swelled over the stove
It plumped down on the floor and on it drove

It swelled and it rolled all over the floor
As the sister witches ran for the door

But then they got an awful fright
For they found the door shut tight

So they hitched up their skirts, jumped up on a chair
And, arms all akimbo, carefully perched there

But still the dough swelled and rose up
Up over the chairs and still did not stop

So they climbed onto the backs of the seats
And scrooged up small and scrunched up their feet

Their eyes got bigger and rounder with fear
Yet still the dough didn't disappear

Same time my knocking kept on through and through
And the witches called out, 'Who's a-knockin? Who?'

My knocking stopped and these words came a-creeping
Through every crack and cranny seeping

'Through stubborn spite you refuse to bend
You are right to believe I am not your friend

I tire now of your tedious talk
You'll never more have strength to walk!'

The witches' legs began to shrink
They looked at each other and began to blink

Their eyes grew large as each turned their head
They were no longer witches, they were owls instead!

And then they heard these words a-creeping
Through the cottage they were a-keeping

'You were wise, my dears, to not open your door
But now you shall live in your house no more

So fly out any window you see
And live your life in a hollow tree'

By this time the dough had risen so high
There was only a little gap up near the sky

Where a window stood, open and ready
So they spread their wings and flew straight and steady

Off into the woods the witch-owls flew
Still calling out 'Who? Who?

Who's that a-knockin? Is it you?
Who's that a-knockin? Whoo! Whoo!'

TALE EIGHT

CROW!

Once upon a time, a scarecrow sat
In a veggie patch in a broad-brimmed hat

Watching the vegetables on the farm
Ensuring the corn came to no harm

Watching corn is tedious and slow
But somebody has to watch them, you know

So he sat there watching and wondering why
'In case the crows should come,' said I

'You must shout Crow! just as loud as you can
And all the villagers, every last man

Will come running uphill, every which way
To help scare those evil crows away'

And so the scarecrow sat in the sun
So bored he almost wished they would come

What if a crow did come before night
Giving the scarecrow an almighty fright
And he shouted Crow! Crow! with all of his might?

What if nobody heard him, nobody came?
Wouldn't that be a terrible shame?

He ought to make sure that they could hear
So the scarecrow leant over a hedge quite near

Until he could see the town down below
And began to shout Crow! Crow! like so

The villagers heard him and snatched up their sticks
Stones and hammers, spades and picks

They came running uphill, just as fast as they could
To drive the crows back into the wood

When they found no crows they had had enough
And, grumbling loudly, went home in a huff

But the scarecrow remained bright and cheery
'I just wanted to make sure you could hear me'

The next day the scarecrow became bored again
He remembered crying Crow! and what fun it'd been...
So he did it again

'Crow!' he shouted, looking quite scared
And up they all ran just as fast as they dared

Slipping and stumbling over rocks and rubble
With their sticks and picks, spade and shovel

'I thought I saw a crow and started to worry
But I guess I was wrong,' he said. 'Sorry'

He wasn't sorry, though, he thought it was fun
To think how easy he had made them all run

So he did it the next day and the next
Until the villagers became perplexed

How many crows were flying about?
How many times would that scarecrow shout?

Meanwhile... not far off in a spot dark and cold
The crows sat watching the events unfold

When they first heard the scarecrow shout their name
Not realising it was all a game

They flew up with a start, trembling with fear
But soon calmed down when no one came near

The second time they stood very still
And although the villagers ran up the hill

No one saw them, no one muttered
And so steadily nearer the big crows fluttered

Each day their position grew a bit stronger
As each time it took the villagers longer

To run up the path with their stones and sticks
Their heavy shovels and heavier picks

And when they all went back down the hill
The crows flew a little bit nearer still
They watched in the shadows and waited until…

Crow! Crow! came the cry from up on high
And the villagers down below heard the cry

But they looked at each other and smiled instead
'We'll teach that scarecrow a lesson,' they said

They shrugged their shoulders with a little smirk
And ignoring the scarecrow, went back to work

'Crow! Crow!' cried the scarecrow at the top of his voice
Surely they'd come, they had no choice

The valley re-echoed with the sound
Caw! Caw! and then there was silence all around
With only feathers upon the ground

The scarecrow stood alone, looking forlorn.
No more crow, no more corn

TALE NINE

THE UGLIEST OF ALL

Henrietta was hideous, more ugly than her sister
Whenever she walked by, everyone would whisper

It didn't matter if she smiled or held herself up tall
They still would whisper 'Henrietta's the *ugliest* of all'

Poor Hetty felt so very sad and tried hard to not cry
She realised she was ugly but she couldn't work out why

She always brushed her teeth and scrubbed her face so clean
Could it be that others were simply being mean?

Henrietta hatched a plan to make herself look nice
She'd borrow her mum's make-up and her curling hair device

But putting on make-up was not as easy as she thought
The curling tongs were tricky and her hair kept getting caught

Her eyelashes were sticky, the earrings too tight
When Hetty looked in the mirror, she gave herself a fright

But in the end she didn't look as bad as she had feared
The ugly Henrietta had almost disappeared

She sashayed and she strutted with her head held high
Imagining the looks as she walked on by

In Mum's high heels she hobbled, trying not to fall
No longer Henrietta, the ugliest of all

But when her mother saw her, she shrieked in alarm
Thinking that someone had done her daughter harm

She couldn't understand why Hetty looked so bad
'Heavens, Henrietta, have you gone quite mad?'

'I'm tired of being ugly,' said Hetty, trying not to bawl
'Everybody says I am the ugliest of all'

Mum smiled at Henrietta, and handed her a tissue
'Silly Henrietta, confusing the issue

No one thinks you're ugly, they don't think that at all
Everybody says you are the *loveliest* of all

You simply didn't hear right,' her Mum said with a laugh
'Now take off all that gunk and give yourself a bath'

When Hetty was herself again, she instantly felt better
'I'm hideous no longer,' smiled the *lovely* Henrietta

TALE TEN

LUCY LAURA LOCKET

Lucy Laura Locket would not cough or sneeze or splutter
She would not shout, she would not whisper, she would not even mutter

Lucy Laura Locket would not say a single word
Well, if she did it's safe to say that no one else had heard

The townsfolk were alarmed and a meeting was declared
Mrs Simpson from the school canteen
Made sandwiches of dried sardines
No expense was spared

Said the eminent Mayor Flutterbye
'We simply must determine why
Miss Lucy Laura Locket will not speak'

Theories had been tossed about
And several citizens surely felt
That Lucy Laura Locket was too meek

'Nonsense,' boomed Miss Bertha Brye
'As her teacher I can testify
Miss Lucy Laura is not shy
It simply is not true

Regardless of the consequence
All efforts must forthwith and hence
Be expended gaining evidence
If only there was something we could do'

Miss Gertie Gert, the most alert
Felt it was almost a cert
That Lucy Laura's voice had disappeared

Then Gertie Gert and Bertha Brye
Both began to wail and cry
For the matter seemed much worse than they had feared

'Voices simply cannot go
It must be somewhere else, you know'
Professor Paradox pontificated

'Has someone summoned Doctor Brown?
A specialist of some renown'
Face upon face began to frown
Til someone wrote the message down
And quickly hurried into town
To fetch the doctor round
And then the townsfolk waited

When at last the Doc arrived
She asked Lucy Laura to open wide
And took a look deep inside
Of Lucy Laura's throat

She ummed and aahed and aahed and ummed
And checked her textbook (well thumbed)
Then quickly grabbed a pen and wrote
Her diagnosis on a note

It read in part and I quote:
'Lucy Laura Locket's throat
Is red raw and sore

Take this potion, once dissolved
And soon the matter will be resolved
Take it easy, have a rest

A lemon drink with honey's best
And to this end I can attest
Your pain will be no more'

The townsfolk cheered and gathered round
Congratulating Doctor Brown

'Three cheers for Doc,' said Bertha Brye
'Hear, hear,' agreed Mayor Flutterbye

With not a dry eye in the hall
Faces turned, one and all
To gaze at Lucy's chin

She opened her mouth and looked about
Said Gertie Gert in a startled shout
'Everybody look out!'
And then…

Lucy shifted her weight from one foot to the other
Smiled at her dad, and kissed her mother

Looked at the Doc, put her hands in her pocket
'Thanks,' said Lucy Laura Locket

TALE ELEVEN

THE SAD, SAD TALE OF ABIGAIL

Part One

Now here's a story of trouble and woe
Why it happened to Abby, I just don't know

But happen it did and twas not so nice
Sadly poor Abby has paid the price

It happened so quickly, as if in a dream
Right out of the blue, if you know what I mean

She went out to a disco, to *Inflation* by chance
Walked onto the floor and started to dance

Her feet moved wildly, as though she were running
And when her hair blew out, she looked quite stunning

The beat was hypnotic, the music quite loud
Abby lifted her head and looked over the crowd

All of a sudden *he* came into view
Romantic, strong, and good-looking too

Thoughts raced through her mind, channelled by fear
What's a nice guy like him doing in here?

Slowly she danced in his general direction
Taking along a friend for protection

With her back to his face, she wiggled her hips
Tossed back her head and moistened her lips

Threw off her shoes, adjusted her dress
All the while thinking, *My God, I'm a mess!*

A tap on her shoulder brought her back with a thud
Biting her lip so hard it drew blood

Slowly she turned, a smile on her face
Oozing with charm, laden with grace

Who would have thought one as lovely as she
Would fall for someone as handsome as he?

But wait, what is this? Shock! Horror! Disgust!
Who stands before her dripping with lust?

Sadly she talks to some odious guy
As slowly her handsome dreamboat walks by

But wait, our story does not end here
One does not give up when one is so near

Our heroine, Abby, returns the next week
No longer hesitant, bewildered or meek

She strides through the door and up to the bar
Surprised that she has made it this far

Her friends all laughed in disparaging tones
Surely she couldn't do it alone?

As they waited outside and watched her go in
All would be losers, only Abby would win

And the prize she was after would surely attest
That Abby only goes after the best

Yes, he was there, acting so cool
But Abby wasn't playing the fool

She was fed up with games and skirting the issue
She straightened her hem and blew her nose on a tissue

Ready for battle she walked onto the floor
It was now or never, of that she was sure

Part Two

It was now or never, she drew a deep breath
To act a fool would be sudden death

She swallowed her fag and stubbed out her drink
A little bit nervous wouldn't you think?

He stood on the floor with a devilish grin
Handsome and worldly and terribly thin

Well to Abby he was, though this may not be so
She's terribly biased, as you probably know

But there's no time for snickers, no time for scorn
For Abby has taken the bull by the horn

She's beside him, behind him, in front if you will
The girl is so nervous her feet won't stay still

But Abby's resourceful and as he dances on by
She leaps into his arms and whisper a 'Hi'

'H-h-hi,' he gasps, regaining his stance
'Did you want me for something or just to dance?'

Abby blushed, Abby gushed, Abby acted the fool
It was hard to be near him and still act so cool

But Abby, you know, doesn't give up her chance
She grabs hold of his hand and they both start to dance

Okay, she concedes, he's hopeless with faces
But I could have done worse if I'd gone down to *Chasers*

He fails to recognise this outstanding figure
I'll just have to approach with a little more vigour

'Remember me?' she managed to squeak
Knowing her chances were looking quite bleak

'I danced with your friend, is he coming tonight?
He's not? Oh well, I guess that's alright'

She snuck into a corner and lowered her voice
He followed her in, he had no choice

She stared into his eyes, her voice barely a whisper
And secretly dreamt that he'd bent down and kissed her

She leant close to his chest, so chunky and sleek
His shirt was quite open so she managed a peek

'It's you that I want,' she had to confess
Slowly his eyes travelled the length of her dress

They moved a bit closer, he was terribly tall
He got her phone number and promised to call

'I have friends who are waiting, I really must go'
Said Abby, her nerves beginning to show

It was a trek to the car but she didn't care
Abby was happy walking on air

To all the best restaurants he'd take her at night
And pay for the meal, much to Abby's delight

Yes, it's true that the first time he kissed her goodnight
She drove into the gutter and got such a fright

Though the car was a mess, Abby seemed not to mind
A love like this was so hard to find

'He's the man of my dreams,' she managed to sigh
'And so much like me, not a bit shy

We have so much fun and always go out
Isn't that what true love is all about?'

And so with those words ringing in our ears
We see the changes in Abby after all these years

For she's happy to daydream and call out his name
Will poor old Abby ever be the same?

Then something happened to burst her bubble
Abby was heading for heartache and trouble

For although the relationship was going so strong
Something would happen to make things go wrong

For one night in a whisper, he managed to speak
'I'm moving to Sydney, I'm leaving next week'

P<small>ART</small> T<small>HREE</small>

Leaving for Sydney? Her heart sank to the ground
So much for the true love she thought she had found

Oh of course she was tempted to follow him there
But leaving her job was too much to bear

And she knew that in Sydney life would be bliss
But her family and friends she surely would miss

'For once in my life I can't follow my heart
I'm sorry, my darling, but here we must part'

Now I'm sure that you think my tale ends here
But you're wrong, for the two lovers still persevere

She'd ring him quite often so he wouldn't forget
The girl left behind much to his regret

And he'd send Abby roses every week
But still her love-life was looking bleak

'He loves me, he loves me,' she'd moan in despair
'Oh why couldn't our love be easy and fair?'

Quickly, too quickly, her roses all died
'I'll get over him soon, I suppose,' Abby lied

Days followed days as they generally do
But Abby still felt lonely and blue

Their talks on the phone were beginning to grow
As the Company's phone bill started to show

To limit the toll they came up with a plan
She'd fly up to Sydney to visit her man

Now although they were happy being together
They knew that this feeling would not last forever

He gave her more roses as they both said goodbye
But she knew back at home her roses would die

If you tell her she's pining, she'll seldom reply
But when you mention his name, there's a tear in her eye

People rarely talk to Abby these days
She seems so set in her melancholy ways

'I know he'll return and together one day
We'll make it work, we'll find a way'

She notices nothing no matter how near
You can talk all you like but she seems not to hear

And if you ask her what flowers she loves to receive
She'll tell you, though I know it seems hard to believe

'Roses,' she'll whisper in a voice soft and hoarse
'Roses, not red ones but DEAD ones, of course'

TALE TWELVE

CINDER-ELLA

Once upon a time as the pages turned
And a log in a fireplace slowly burned

Ella sat by the fire, reading a book
Her face and hair covered in soot

She spent her days scrubbing and cooking
And all of her nights reading a booking…

I mean a book, look, she was practically a slave
With a step-mother who would rant and rave

'Clean up! Pick up! Mop up! Scrub!
Get to work, you worthless grub!'

Ella was forced to do all the chores
From dusting the ceiling to scrubbing the floors

You know how this goes, do I need to spell it?
Do you need to be hit on the head with a mallet?

Ella's step-mum was horrid and hairy
And her voice was more than a little scary

'You need sense knocked into your noggin
What you deserve is another floggin!'

As you can guess, Ella was sad
When she thought of her life, it made her feel bad

She didn't need this aggravation
And a life chock-full of limitation

She wanted to live in a fairytale world
Where dreams and fantasies unfurled

With one hand holding onto a book
She continued to scrub and clean and cook

Of course her step-mum seethed in a rage
With every turning of the page

And that is how Ella survived
Until the day a letter arrived

Every maiden in the land
Is eligible for Prince Harry's hand

A formal ball, tomorrow night
Will help the Prince find his Miss Right

'At last my prince has come,' said Portia
She was the step-mum's ugly daughter

'Prince Harry is meant to be my mister'
Said Prudence, Portia's ugly sister

'Who cares?' said Ella. 'What a bore
Who cares what Prince Harry is looking for?'

Portia and Prudence wailed and whined
'A man like that is hard to find!'

'Good,' said Ella, 'then I won't even look'
And promptly put her nose in a book

This tale would have ended as it began
Except Ella's step-mum had a plan

'My girls must look their very best
So Cinder-Ella will get them dressed

To arrive in style, they'll ride with the Duchess
And Ella will add the final touches'

Ella sat in the coach as the girls went inside
There was literally nowhere else to hide

It's enough to make a poor girl cry
But then a horse-drawn carriage went by

The horse stopped, it's hooves a-clatter
How it got there, it doesn't matter

The door burst open and girls burst out
With more than one excited shout

It was indeed a sight to behold
A gaggle of girls, both young and old

In a flurry of taffeta, sparkles and chintz
All intent on snagging a prince

'He's mine! He's mine!' they said on the trot
But the driver laughed and said, 'What rot!'

Have you guessed who she could be?
You're right, of course – it's me!

Dressed in black, with my hair all wild
I looked at Ella and then I smiled

'Isn't this all a hoot
And over a silly boy to boot'

Ella told me what she thought
She figured it would count for nought

'It's a waste of time, there is no doubt
I don't know what all the fuss is about'

I laughed at that and tossed my hair
As you can imagine, it went everywhere

'The fuss, my dear, is all the fun
It isn't about finding "the one"

It's living your life, true and sound
And refusing to be pushed around

You've got the second, now you need the first
A life half-lived is a life half-cursed'

I knew what was to become of her fate
And didn't think that Ella should wait

'Escape can come in many guises
You must grab your chance as it arises'

I held the coach door open wide
And Ella simply stepped inside

When her wicked step-mum left the ball
She couldn't find Ella anywhere at all

She searched everywhere she could think to look
But all she found was an open book

And there on the page that was starting to curl
Was a picture of a happy girl

With a grin as wide as an open umbrella
And she looked the spitting image of Ella

TALE THIRTEEN

PRINCESS POLLY AND THE PEA

Once upon a time, far across the sea
    There was a Princess and a pea

    Princess Polly was serene
      The pea was… green

Now this pea possessed magical powers
And stayed fresh on a plate for hours and hours

    And anyone who ate this pea
  Would become as magical as can be

    The pea, through the hands of fate
      Ended upon on Polly's plate

It seems her troubles did begin
When she journeyed into the Kingdom of Grim

The Palace held a formal ball
And gave the Princess Polly a call

It was hoped that Prince Harry, handsome and strong
Could provide a love lasting and long

And cause dear Polly to swoon and sway
And the Prince would marry her straight away

Polly's dad was not fond of his daughter
And didn't love her as much as he ought-a

So he sent her over the treacherous sea
And that's how she ended up with that pea

At suppertime, the Prince found his seat
And then began to eat and eat

It wasn't the best start to their dating
As Polly sat around just waiting

For her palate, being so refined
Made some ingredients hard to find

In fact it didn't look so great
With only a pea upon the plate

But things were about to get much worse
For I'm afraid I did a little curse

Disguised as a servant, I served the plate
Thus sealing Princess Polly's fate

As I passed the table laden with bread
Naughty thoughts filled my head

Thought one: I must reverse the plan
Polly cannot get her man

This pea with all of its amazing power
Must be mine within the hour

Which led me to thought number two and three
Who would notice if I grabbed the pea?
Who would even be looking at me?

And without even bothering to wait
I took the pea right off the plate

Into my mouth, the pea was popped
As I pretended it had been dropped

And, being obviously more than able
Placed the empty plate upon the table

Polly waved the plate away
And was right and royally heard to say

'I couldn't eat another bite
I think I'll turn in for the night'

At this the Prince arched his brow
And I knew the time to act was now

I wished I was in Polly's place
With Prince Harry staring into my face

No sooner had my wish been wished
Than courtesy of the pea, now squished

The switch was made, our souls were swapped
So fast that both my ears were popped

Through space and time our souls did switch
Til I was a princess and Polly a witch

To the outside eye, no one could tell
That Polly was under a magic spell

At first she felt her spirit soar
Til she was in herself no more

She saw her body in the seat
But I was squatting in her feet

When the Prince asked if her meal was good
Polly didn't answer as she should

For it was my words that carried weight
As I looked down at the empty plate

'I can't be sure but something lacked
That rotten chef should be sacked

The pea was too wrinkled for my taste
I'm afraid the meal was a ghastly waste'

The Prince was quickly taken aback
By such a vicious verbal attack

But he liked my spunk and good looks too
So he ignored the rest, as men often do

He got down on one knee, as best as was able
And picked up a pea that had rolled under the table

Then he got back up and proposed we wed
Thought I don't remember what he said

Now the real Polly, it transpires
Was watching all this through my eyes

She saw her chosen choose another
And under her breath she said, 'Oh bother!'

Her heart was broken, as expected
As in her place, I accepted

And as I sighed and started to swoon
The Prince resolved to get a tic-tac soon

Then he whisked me away to a room in the Palace
Leaving poor Polly feeling jealous

Trapped as a witch, disguised as a slave
She didn't know quite how to behave

So I, disguised as the Princess Bride
Invited Polly along for the ride

She can be my maid, what are friends for?
And trapped as a slave, this is what she saw

The richest jewels and softest furs
Yes, all the things that should have been hers

Were now all mine to have and to hold
All of the gems and all of the gold

But best of all, it has to be said
Were twenty-one mattresses on a bed

I know it sounds a little extreme
But at first I was incredibly keen

Until I went to turn in for the night
And realised all was not quite right

The whole thing looked like an overgrown hedge
As a ladder was placed at the utmost edge

I clambered up and carefully perched
For a stable spot, I frantically searched

The Prince stood below watching all of this
Then said, 'Goodnight,' and blew a kiss

As soon as he left, I climbed back down
'It's all yours, Polly,' I said with a frown

And forced our luckless heroine
To scramble up and snuggle in

In the morning, the Prince thought he saw
The servant in bed, the Princess on the floor

And, wanting to know what it's all about
'What's this?' he demanded with a shout

He woke me up and, feeling grumpy
'That bed,' I said, 'was much too lumpy

My servant had to take my place'
(I was still disguised in Polly's face)

'Twenty-one mattresses on a bed?
I was half terrified out of my head

You stupid oaf, I hate you so!'
(I'm not a morning person, you know)

The Prince was crushed, his dreams were shattered
But I was really all that mattered

I grabbed the gowns, then looked about
Found the jewels, and stormed on out

And the Prince was left in no doubt
As to how this 'princess' really felt

Well, how was he to know instead
That the real Princess was still in bed

And thinking she was just a slave
Dismissed her presence with a wave

'Get up, slob,' is what he said
And Polly nearly fell off the bed

'How rude,' she said, feeling flushed
'I do beg your pardon,' the poor Prince blushed

For as the sun shone in the room
Dissipating all the gloom

There was a switch, a rearrange
And, yes, it felt a little strange

Instead of souls hurtling through space
It was our bodies trading place

A hiss, a pop, a shake, a sheen
And all was as it once had been

Princess Polly was still in place
And now staring out of her usual face

She touched her cheek, let out a sigh
'I'm me again,' she said, 'tis I'

Prince Harry did a double take
And saw he'd made a huge mistake

'I meant no harm, Princess,' he said
'Do you need help getting out of bed?'

'That's better,' said Polly, 'far more tact
And I do need help, as a matter of fact'

'And how did you sleep?' the Prince enquired
Noticing that she looked a bit tired

'It's strange,' she said, 'who would have guessed
That with all those layers, I'd still be stressed

I tossed and turned all night long
Something about that bed was wrong

I'm afraid I felt under attack
As something hard dug into my back'

At this the Prince wept with joy
Well, he is a sensitive new-age boy

'At last,' he said, 'you've passed the test
I've finally found a true Princess

Only skin so soft and sweet
Would feel something hard beneath the sheet

You are the only one for me'
And he pulled out a green pea!

TALE FOURTEEN

PRUNELLA

This is the story of Aunt Prunella…
Who lives in a lovely house by the sea
Near me

Every day, whilst others slept
She scrubbed and dusted, fluffed and swept

Then she would open her curtains wide
And let the sunshine stream inside

Finally, she brushed her hair so thin
And held it back with a bobby-pin

Because, and this is a handy lesson
Self-grooming gives a good impression

Every day was always the same
Nobody called, nobody came

And so Prunella kept herself busy
Working so hard she made herself dizzy

Sweeping, cleaning, dusting the dust
Polishing the silver, removing the rust

Scrubbing, rubbing, waxing and waning
Sanding the floor and then re-staining

Primping, preening and then more cleaning
Until Prunella's house was gleaming

But still each day was the same
Nobody ever, ever came

Out of the window Prunella would stare
Until she died in her rocking chair

It happened one day
As she faded away

Rock… rock… rock…
Stop

Then Prunella's grand-nieces, Mildread and Maudelin
Who looked like they'd overdosed on laudanum

THE WITCH'S TALE · 95

Moved into the house by the sea
Near me

They were noisy and messy and so much fun
They howled at the moon and glared at the sun

They danced at midnight, rarely seen
And never had any time to clean

Maudelin was busy casting spells
Dropping coins into wishing wells

Tampering with the lighthouse locks
So that ships might dash against the rocks

There was food to poison, bills thrown away
And all those chores we do every day

Like beds to unmake, washing to undo
And boiling up a witch's brew

Maudelin was busy and did such a lot
That she never had time to clean even a spot

Well, the floors got swept, I have to say
When an evil spirit was banished away

And toilets were scrubbed, it has to be said
When Maudelin shoved in somebody's head

And though this happens surprisingly often
I still think Maudelin is starting to soften

It's very rare that she will flush
Or use their head as a toilet brush

And if you think Mildread picks up the slack
Let me advise you to take that back

If you go to the dead end of town and stop
You'll see Mildread's Potions & Lotions shop

And it's there that Mildread reigns supreme
On all things sick that can't be seen

An allergic reaction and off she'd dash
Curing another unspeakable rash

And she never, ever could resist
A juicy boil or puss-filled cyst

(Well, who can?)

The house naturally wasn't spotless or clean
And it certainly didn't glisten or gleam

But there were lots of visitors, I have to say
And they came almost every day

Some came to conjure, some came to cast
Some to banish back to the past

Some to summon from the great unknown
But nobody came to clean their home

Now I might have embellished their witchy ways
And the things they did to fill their days

But believe me when I say to you
That no one ever cleaned their loo

And I can honestly say for certain
That no one ever opened a curtain

But Aunt Prunella, though she had died
Had not passed on to the other side

Her spirit remained, sight unseen
In a house that was sadly now unclean

She wondered what her nieces were doing
Letting her home go to rack and ruin

But they could not see Prunella at all
And not because of her ghostly pall

The girls see spirits all of the time
Ignoring one is not a crime

But their lives were too hectic to smell the roses
That Prunella was shoving under their noses

They were too busy flying about on their broom
To notice Prunella in the room

But now that Prunella was dead
She saw things with a clearer head

She saw the mess, the muck, the dust
Brass unpolished turned to rust

It's enough to make a saint feel snappy
Prunella clearly was not happy

She tried to show in many ways
That in her eyes grime never pays

She rattled windows and, feeling bold
Blew through keyholes icy cold

She moved the furniture, creaked the floor
And once she even slammed a door

But the sisters didn't hear her pleas
They simply felt more at ease

Until one day Prunella cracked
And in a frenzy she attacked

First the washing on the floor
Then the capes behind the door

And frankly she had had enough
Of bottles filled with freaky stuff

She cleaned them out with antiseptic spray
And then she put them all away

(But nobody noticed)

So the next day she began again
Clearing out the sisters' den

She scrubbed and dusted, polished and buffed
I hate to say it, but cushions were fluffed

She opened the spider-web curtains wide
And let the sunshine stream inside

(And now they noticed)

Mildread shouted, Maudelin fumed
Lots of chocolate was consumed

Each blamed the other, as you can see
And no one bothered asking me

They argued so much that it was too late
To change the house's pristine state

Prunella took it as a sign
That all her cleaning was just fine

And so, I hate to admit
But she kept on cleaning it

Mildread and Maudelin soon worked out
That a kindly spirit was flying about

Alas, a spirit who liked to clean
It's enough to make a poor girl scream
(I think you know what I mean)

And then one day things came to a head
Between the living and the dead

It began with a hammering at the door
Which the sisters simply chose to ignore

Something was wrong, I could tell
So I went next door and rang the bell

I walked in the house and felt a change
Things seemed different, a little strange

A gentle breeze blew soft and sweet
Through windows clean and curtains neat

The scent of flowers still in bloom
Gently wafted in the room

Furniture gleamed, glasses glistened
I tried to warn them but nobody listened

So I stood upon their shiny floor
And stared at the plaque upon the door
(That was what the hammering was for)

It said one word: PRUNELLA

(Aargh!)

This is the story of Aunt Prunella…
A *ghost* who lives in a lovely house by the sea
Near me

For more adventures with Mildread and Maudelin
And their ghostly Aunt Prunella, be sure to read
The Bellwether Rules for the Dead
{A ghost story}

But for now…

Close your eyes and remember my tale
   Face the dark and lift the veil

   Corpses dead may rot away
   But legends live another day

I am the breath that cannot die
I am the gleam in the warrior's eye

   I am the Princess and the pea
The beginning and the end is me

When wars are ended and stories told
   And youth is wasted on the old

   I shall return triumphant, then
The witch's tale shall begin again

Kerry Mitchell

Also Available

From One Extreme to the Other
{A book of poetry}

Coming Soon

The Bellwether Rules for the Dead
{A ghost story}

And

Theodora van Runkle
{Be careful what you wish for}

www.ingramcontent.com/pod-product-compliance
Lightning Source LLC
Chambersburg PA
CBHW032045290426
44110CB00012B/953